The Mustard Seed Effect

A Memoir of Pain, Survival, Healing, and Faith.

Parker J.

This book is a work of nonfiction based on the author's
life experiences. Some names,
descriptions, identifying characteristics, and other details
may have been changed to
protect the privacy of individuals mentioned in this book.

First edition, 2026

Author: Parker J.
Cover design by Clint English
Interior formatting by Author

ISBN: 979-8-234-06153-9

Printed in the United States of America

Contents

Part One: *The Foundation*..1

Chapter 1: The Hands That Raised Me....................2

Chapter 2: Our Apartment................................8

Chapter 3: The Family House............................10

Chapter 4: The Discovery................................12

Chapter 5: The Island...................................14

Chapter 6: The Little Trailer on "The Front".......16

Chapter 7: Elementary School...........................18

Chapter 8: Friend Turned Sister........................19

Chapter 9: Dance Battles & Rapping.....................21

Part Two: *Cracks In the Ground*.........................23

Chapter 10: A Breath of Fresh Air......................24

Chapter 11: Let Freedom Ring...........................25

Chapter 12: No More Bullets............................28

Chapter 13: Teen Court.................................30

Chapter 14: Hospital & Cartoons........................31

Chapter 15: The Leather Heart..........................33

Chapter 16: The Clinic.................................35

Part Three: *Falling and Fighting*.......................37

Chapter 17: Prove Them Wrong...........................38

Chapter 18: Mistaken Identity..........................39

Chapter 19: He Spoke to Me.............................45

Chapter 20: Construction Life..........................48

Chapter 21: Pre-Trial Intervention.....................52

Chapter 22: Unfortunate Circumstances..................53

Chapter 23: A Settled Blessing.........................54

Part Four: *Becoming* 55

    Chapter 24: Entrepreneur 56

    Chapter 25: The White Dove 57

    Chapter 26: My First Foundation 58

    Chapter 27: Water Revival and Spiritual Encounters 60

Part Five: *Reckoning and Healing* 65

    Chapter 28: Consequences 66

    Chapter 29: Access and Egress 68

    Chapter 30: The Mustard Seed Effect 70

    Chapter 31: Where's Your Work? 73

    Chapter 32: Healing: I Know Who I Am 75

    Chapter 33: God Gives Us Free Will: What Is to Blame? 77

    Chapter 34: Forgiveness 80

    Chapter 35: The Right Way to Love 85

Poems: *Words From the Wise* 88

    Promiscuity Without the Promise 89

    All It Takes 90

    The Love of Fire: Let It Burn 91

    Emulsions: Battle Of the Flesh and Holy Spirit ... 92

Acknowledgements

Most importantly, I give thanks to God for carrying me through every trial, lesson, and season of growth. Without His love, grace, and mercy this story would not have been possible.

I would also like to thank my mom who encouraged me to be authentic and be open about my life. Her unwavering support throughout many years helped me become the woman I am today.

Lastly, I want to thank the influential people in my life: my Church of the King family, my children, brother, aunts, cousins, Dr. Davis, the Lewis/Thomas family.

Introduction

Hello, I am Parker J., the author of the book you are about to read. First, I would like to thank each of you for being a part of my healing journey by allowing my story to help you heal as well. I pray that someone finds peace after reading it. Writing my testimony is my way of helping others overcome adversity and experience transformation. Many of you have faced similar circumstances—incarceration, sexual abuse, and repeated failures. I believe that sharing my story can help prevent your faith from weakening. Greatness happens to those who believe.

As a mother of six beautiful children, the need to heal became especially important. Healing from past trauma is essential when raising children. Carrying hurtful and unwanted baggage only became a hindrance in my role as a mother. Showing up every day, internally disappointed with my life choices, caused me a great deal of stress. During the writing process, I experienced feelings of panic and grief. I had to revisit everything—the good and bad. However, I knew I had to complete this process so I could become a voice for those who are walking in darkness or searching for the light. My deepest desire is to bridge the gap between the two because I have experienced both sides.

The phrase "everything happens for a reason" truly encapsulates my life. I was reluctant to share my story due to feelings of shame and embarrassment. Most of all, I did not want to face the reality of my truth. But even a small amount of faith, the size of a mustard seed, helped me uncover what I had suppressed for years. I had faith that writing would help me heal. Faith that my experiences would leave a lasting impact on those seeking encouragement. Faith that every decision I've made—past, present, and future—would serve as a beacon of hope for the lost or discouraged. I am often reminded that creating a beautiful painting is not always a beautiful process for the artist. What may feel like chaos to the creator can become something meaningful to the viewer. Being the artist of my own life forced me to confront the ugliness, turmoil, and carelessness within myself, while others only saw the finished product. Still, I was determined to be authentic. That authenticity helped me understand what it truly means to become a faithful believer. The only way to do that is by acknowledging every flaw, every splatter, every unintended brushstroke, every imperfection. Those very imperfections are what make the final picture meaningful.

If you had met me at different points in my life, you may not have recognized me as the same person. There was a time when I was just trying to survive, navigating instability, making decisions I didn't fully understand, and searching for love in places that only left me empty. I became a mother while I was still a child myself. I made choices that cost me deeply—emotionally, mentally, and professionally. At one point, I lost everything I had worked so hard to build. And yet, I am still here. This book is not just a story about what I've been through, it is a story about what I overcame. It is about accountability, growth, faith, and the power of choosing differently, even after getting it wrong. There were moments in my life when I felt stuck in cycles I didn't know how to break. I believed certain things were just "how life was." But over time, I realized that while I could not change where I came from, I could change how my story continued.

Faith became the foundation of that change. Not perfect faith—but the kind that starts small. The kind that grows in the middle of confusion, pain, and uncertainty. The kind that carries you when you don't even realize you're being carried.

This book is for anyone who has ever:

• felt like they were repeating the same mistakes
• questioned their worth
• wondered if it was too late to change
• or felt defined by their past

I want you to know that it's not. Your past may explain you, but it does not have to define you. Every chapter you are about to read is a piece of my journey—the good, the painful, and the lessons in between. I share it not because I have it all figured out, but because I know what it feels like to be lost and what it takes to find your way back. If there is one thing I hope you take from my story, it is this: Change is possible. All it takes is faith the size of a mustard seed.

Part One: *The Foundation*

Chapter 1: The Hands That Raised Me

Mama

Mama, the most beautiful woman on planet Earth. Wearing red lipstick and polished nails were her signature. Her tall, model-like figure, loving spirit, and radiant smile defined her. I remember her bright white teeth and her mushroom haircut. She reminded me of a blend of Whitney Houston and Toni Braxton. She never missed an opportunity to keep herself up. Her salon visits were routine, and she always carried herself as if she were runway ready. Her beauty was striking— the kind that drew attention without trying. I once told my great-aunt that I got my beauty from my mom. She laughed and said, "Oh no, you could never be pretty like your mom," before going on and on about how gorgeous Mama was. Her words did not offend me. Instead, they made me adore my mother even more. Mama's beauty reached far beyond her outward appearance. There was a softness and grace in her heart that made her even more beautiful. In so many ways, her spirit reminded me of my grandmother's.

My mom has always had a profound sense of humor. She would jokingly tell my brother and me that her head was pounding. We were so naïve that we believed she was in serious pain. She would call us into her room to help make her headache go away, telling us the "blood" had risen to the top of her head. She would ask us to rub her temples so the blood could go back down. Being as caring as we were, we got to work immediately. My brother took the left side, and I took the right. In a panic, we rubbed her temples, believing we were saving her life. After twenty minutes, we would ask if the blood had gone down. She would point slightly lower on her head to show us progress. Another twenty minutes

later, we would ask again. Sometimes she would fall
asleep, but we would wake her, thinking she was
drifting away. Eventually, we caught on. We stopped
waking her and would sneak out of the room—until
she called us back in to repeat the cycle. Yes, the
"blood" always went back to the top of her head. Yes,
we would get exhausted. But we loved believing we
were taking care of her. In reality, she just wanted
help falling asleep.

Everything with her was routine. She worked
the day shift, but we would often beat her home. She
always made sure we had an after-school snack,
usually a candy bar or ice cream. Those were the good
days.

We were raised in church and attended every
Sunday. My mom and grandmother served as ushers.
My brother and I sang in the choir, and I was on the
praise dance team. We loved going to church.
Watching my mom in her beautiful white dress was
something special. Our grandmother would pass us
peppermints to help us stay awake. I didn't always
understand the sermons, but we knew the Ten
Commandments. Mama made sure of that. She
showed affection in her own unique ways—like gently
pinching our noses because they were a bit more
pronounced. It reminded me of the scene in *Face Off*,
when the father slides his hand down his daughter's
face to show love and recognition. Mama constantly
reassured us of her love. She was sensitive,
empathetic, and never afraid to show emotion.

Pops

I often refer to my dad as Pops because of his
long gray beard. My dad has always been involved in
our lives. He still calls and checks on my family
consistently. Growing up with a man like him was
truly a blessing. He has always been laid-back. I can

recall my dad giving us a spanking only once before we became teenagers. His slender build and deep, stern voice were usually all we needed for correction. He once told me that we respected him because he started disciplining us at a noticeably early age. While I wouldn't say we feared him, we definitely knew not to step out of line by the time we were three and four years old. I remember when he and Mama were married. We lived in a single-wide trailer on Mississippi Street, with our daycare within walking distance. Mama would either pick us up, or we would walk home with a staff member. Pops was always working. I remember him coming home looking completely worn out, like he had just gone several rounds in a boxing match. I'm sure that's part of the reason I developed a strong work ethic and appreciation for the manufacturing industry. Eventually, my parents divorced. Pops would pick us up on the weekends and take us to a different house. He used to comb my hair into pigtails—though they would stick straight up. Looking back, I couldn't be prouder of him for trying. My hair may not have been perfect, but it was good enough for him to take us out to the nearest burger spot.

The divorce became more real to my brother and me when we stopped spending nights on Mississippi Street together as a family. There were even times when my parents got their schedules mixed up, and neither one picked us up from daycare. We ended up spending the night at the owner's house, both of them thinking the other had us. We laugh about it now. Pops made sure we always had what we needed. He handled shopping for all our clothes—school, summer, and winter. We would fill up baskets with clothes and shoes, and he was a firm believer in layaway. Because of that, we always had a steady rotation of clothes for every season. Mama just wasn't much of a shopper, but Pops never dropped the ball.

He worked incredibly hard for us. He was a resolute sandblaster and painter who rarely missed a day of work. He woke up early, stayed consistent, and never complained. His blue lunch bucket was always packed with peanuts, a sandwich, and a Pepsi, along with a pack of Big Red gum. He prepared everything the night before. Pops was always ready.

Stepmother

I genuinely believe God handpicked her for my dad. She is everything I could have hoped for in a stepmother. I'm convinced my dad was the one pursuing her, because she seemed completely content minding her own business and living her life. She has always been a modest, independent woman. Saying she had her life together before meeting my dad would be an understatement. She had no children, owned her own home and property, and was already a manager at her job. Everything about her was neat, organized, and well-kept, including her home. My stepmom worked for one of the most well-known fried chicken restaurants in the world and had already been there for nearly eighteen years when she met my dad. She took her job very seriously, and her more than forty-year tenure speaks volumes about her dedication and discipline.

Despite having no children of her own, she embraced the responsibility of caring for us. I remember one weekend when my dad had to work while we were staying with him. She came over—his girlfriend at the time—to babysit us. My brother and I peeked at her from behind the wall while she sat in the living room. She had such a serious and strict presence that we were too shy to approach her at first. Eventually, we warmed up. She makes the best spaghetti. Between that and the endless supply of chicken from her job, we were never hungry when we were with her. She knew exactly how we liked our meals—even down to the condiments. When she and my dad moved in together, everything changed for the better. We had our own room and bathroom, and for the first time, we felt truly settled. It felt like home—like heaven.

Her love has never wavered. She never treated us like stepchildren. As I got older, I often wondered how a woman without children could become such an important part of our lives. She is the type to laugh and cry deeply. Making her laugh was always my goal, especially because she carried herself with such seriousness. She didn't play around and was extremely strict. She would wake us up early during the fall to rake leaves, trim hedges, and clean the yard. She instilled discipline and a strong work ethic in us— lessons that have stayed with me.

Big Broski

My big brother and I are extremely close. We are only eleven months apart—yes, you can do the math on that. Although he is older, I have always felt like the big sister. Let me explain. Whenever he had issues with boys at school, he wouldn't say he was going to get a male cousin or friend—he would say he was going to get me. I acted more like a protector because of my maturity and toughness. Now, how exactly was I supposed to fight boys? Honestly, I'm not sure—but I tried. Or maybe they just didn't want to hit a girl. Either way, I chose to believe they were scared of me. He wasn't a coward—far from it. He just had a soft heart and didn't like hurting people, especially given his size. He was much taller than his peers but never used it to his advantage. He had been so loved and nurtured by our mom that fighting just wasn't in him. So, little big sister stepped in. He would even warn his girlfriends, saying, "Don't mess over me, or I'll call my sister."

Because of his asthma attacks, I naturally became his protector and caretaker when we were alone. I constantly checked on him to make sure he was okay and breathing properly. Even though I watched over him, he also looked out for me, especially as we got older. One day, it seemed like he had just shot up and became taller than our six-foot-tall mom. That's when his "big brother" instincts really kicked in. I wasn't allowed to date or even show interest in any of his friends—and they definitely knew not to cross any lines with me. He didn't play about his little sister.

To this day, I still call him my teddy bear. He towers over me and even went on to play college football. But despite his size, he is as gentle as can be, with the biggest heart. When he hugs me, it feels like being wrapped up by the softest, kindest giant. He calls me just to hear me crack jokes so he can laugh. Sometimes he'll ask me to repeat something just so he can laugh all over again. We definitely get our sense of humor from Mama. I love him more than words can express.

Chapter 2: Our Apartment

When I was five years old, I remember moving into an apartment down the street from my grandparents' house. My brother and I were so excited. My mom took us there to see it beforehand. It was her first home after divorcing my dad, following a brief time living with my grandmother. I quickly made new friends, boys, and girls of all backgrounds. I remember becoming friends with a boy of Spanish descent who had a small crush on me. At one point, he even tried to dunk me under the water in the community pool, thinking it was a way to flirt or get my attention. I also met a little girl who had a brother with a similar age gap as me and my brother. We were adventurous—we jumped fences and explored everything around us. I still have a scar on my side from getting caught on one. We had so much fun.

The school we attended was outside the city limits and very calm. Our mom believed strongly in routines, so our days were structured. One rule she enforced strictly was that we were never to open the door for anyone when she wasn't home—no matter the situation. If someone knocked, we were to call her. Even when our aunt or grandmother came to check on us, we spoke to them through the door. That's how seriously we followed her rule—until Hurricane Andrew. We didn't fully understand what was happening. We only knew school was canceled. Like kids, we went outside and played in the floodwaters. Thankfully, we weren't hurt, but someone saw us and called our aunt. When she came, ironically we initially refused to open the door because we were trying to follow our mom's rule. Eventually, she got in—and we got a well-deserved whipping.

Despite everything, we made so many memories there. My brother and I still talk about the shows we used to watch. After school, we would come home, lock the door, do our homework, and watch Nickelodeon until our mom got home from work. One morning, we were awakened by loud banging. "Boom! Boom! Boom!" "This is the Village Fire Department!" a firefighter shouted. My mom jumped out of bed and ran to the front door. We followed her. "Everyone, get out now!" he yelled. We grabbed what we could and rushed outside. To our right, a nearby building was engulfed in flames. The next day, my mom told us that our apartment had caught fire as well. The building burned to the ground, and we lost everything.

At the time, we didn't know how deeply it affected her. She kept smiling, hiding her pain from us. But from my perspective, it felt like everything began to go downhill after that. We eventually moved into what we called the "red projects," named after the red brick exterior. It was actually the better of the two project homes we would later live in. Despite losing everything, our bond grew stronger. We stayed enrolled in the same elementary school by using our grandparents' address, since they still lived down the street from where our apartment once stood. Our mom would drop us off there so we could catch the bus. There was an ice cream shop near our new apartment, and Mama always made sure we had something sweet waiting in the freezer after school.

Things remained somewhat stable—until the day her sister came to visit. I was too young to understand why they locked themselves in the room and wouldn't let us in. But that day marked the beginning of the most difficult chapter of our lives.

Chapter 3: The Family House

Growing up in the country generated so many good memories. We spent a lot of time at our grandmother's house. She had a very distinct laugh that I can still hear to this day. Every morning before school, most of her grandchildren would be there. She would prepare coffee milk and buttered toast for us before we caught the bus. We would sit at the bar, dipping our toast into our coffee milk and enjoying every bite. Behind the house was a pig pen. My grandparents were farmers, raising pigs and chickens. In the evenings, we would be dropped off there again, finish our homework, and eat her savory red beans and rice before Mama came to pick us up after work.

On days we didn't have school, we played outside from morning until night. There was no going in and out unless we needed to use the bathroom or eat. Other than that, we stayed outside all day— playing or sitting on the swing hanging from the tree. It was so peaceful. The quiet and the sound of birds chirping felt like music. When we were inside, we often watched *The Color Purple* with her. She loved that movie and played it all the time. Also living there was my youngest aunt. There was only about a ten-year age gap between us, so I never really called her "Aunt." We called her by her name. I was her little shadow—wherever she went, I followed. She loved to make us laugh and scream with her scary jokes. One time, when Mama made a quick stop at Grandma's, my brother and I stayed in the car. Out of nowhere, she came running from behind the house wrapped in a sheet. We screamed and cried, thinking she was a ghost. She laughed so hard once she scared us. She was very convincing and always told spooky stories with a straight face. She once convinced me that dancing to "God Bless America" meant I was possessed by a demon. I think I was the most gullible out of all of us. She would even point at my forehead and tell me I had horns growing out of it. Everyone would join in, pointing and agreeing. I honestly believe she joked with me the most because I was—and still am—her favorite niece. She treated me like a little sister. Trips to the mall and quick store runs with her were always fun. When she graduated high school and left to play college basketball, I cried for days. Not long after, when I was about eight years old, my grandmother moved out of state and remarried, leaving the family home empty for years.

Chapter 4: The Discovery

I remember being around eight years old when I first sensed that something in Mama had changed. It was as though something had settled over her that did not match the loving spirit I had always known. She did not seem like herself. I was a very observant child—curious, watchful, and often aware of more than people realized—so it did not take me long to notice that something was wrong.

At that age, I did not have the words to understand what she was facing, nor could I fully grasp the weight of the battle she was carrying. I only knew that some of her ways no longer reflected the values she had instilled in us or the things I had learned in church. Watching Mama slowly seem unlike herself was deeply unsettling to me. Looking back, I can now see that her struggle was only beginning.

Because I loved her so much, I never hesitated to ask what was wrong. Sometimes she would answer in ways that confused me, and other times she would not answer at all. There were moments when it felt like she was carrying something heavy and unseen, something that was pulling her away from herself and from the people who loved her most. Little by little, her demeanor changed, and she began to withdraw from those closest to her.

As the months passed, I began to understand that Mama was battling addiction. Even so, she continued working and doing her best to function through a struggle that was much greater than I could comprehend at the time. My brother and I grew more and more concerned for her well-being, often interrupting her isolation simply because we wanted to make sure she was okay. Over time, our concern sometimes turned into anger, not because we stopped loving her, but because we did not know how to make sense of what we were witnessing.

Even in the middle of that confusion, we still respected her. We worried constantly when she was not home, afraid that something terrible might happen to her. But ours was not the only family living through that kind of pain. Many children around us were witnessing similar struggles in their own homes, and each of us learned to carry it in different ways. Looking back, it felt as though so many families in Abbeville were under the weight of the same kind of suffering. During our visits with our dad, we hid much of what was happening. We loved our mother deeply, and we did not want to leave her. In many ways, we felt responsible for protecting her, even though we were only children ourselves. As we grew older, the weight of our circumstances began to shape us, quietly pushing us into survival mode.

Chapter 5: The Island

Around the age of eight, everything began to change even more. Because of our unfortunate circumstances, one of my mom's siblings insisted on allowing us to move in with them. My dad agreed, leaving us with no choice. I want to believe my dad didn't fully understand what was happening. I don't think he realized how serious my mom's condition had become.

We moved in with my aunt. Although I can appreciate someone stepping in, living there did not bring me peace. I felt isolated, disconnected, and alone. I went from seeing my mom every few days to only seeing her every couple of weeks. There were moments that looked like a normal childhood—playing outside, chasing the ice cream truck, jumping on trampolines, playing football, pretending to be Power Rangers. But underneath it all, something wasn't right. I call that place "the island" because that's exactly how it felt—cut off, quiet, and unseen. Although the home itself appeared stable, what I experienced there would affect me for the rest of my life. In the early mornings, while everyone else was asleep, I was repeatedly violated in a way no child should ever experience. It became something I began to anticipate—not because I accepted it, but because I had no control over it. I tried to protect myself in the only ways I knew how. I would switch sleeping positions with my female cousin, hoping to avoid being targeted. But what I feared most happened— someone else was hurt too. I remember hearing her cry out, and even now, that moment stays with me.

That experience brought a deep sense of guilt, even though I was just a child trying to survive. This didn't begin there—it had started earlier when I was younger.

I stayed silent. Not because I didn't want help, but because I was afraid—afraid of what would happen if I spoke up, afraid of not being believed, and afraid of the consequences. So, I carried it alone. I internalized everything—the confusion, the shame, the fear. Over time, it began to shape how I saw myself. My self-worth slowly diminished, and I started to believe things about myself that no child should ever believe. Those feelings stayed with me for years.

Chapter 6: The Little Trailer on "The Front"

Mr. Mark was much shorter than Mama—maybe even half her size. He lived in a small two-bedroom trailer in an area known as "the front." There was a family-owned mini mart nearby that sold everything—boudin, hot links, pickled pig feet, and all kinds of snacks. When we first met him, he rode a bicycle. Later, he got an older car. Even though Mama was still struggling, he loved her and helped keep us together. In my opinion, he was the kindest man she had ever been with. He was involved in our lives. Mr. Mark made the best sweet potato pies and pecan candy. His brown gravy and smothered turkey wings were unforgettable. He was known around town for his cooking. He would let me and my brother help in the kitchen, especially with preparing pies. With the money he made, he would give us a few dollars to go to the store and buy snacks. He also had asthma, just like my brother. Sometimes they even shared treatments when one ran out of medication. Because I was used to helping my brother, I was always alert and ready if Mr. Mark needed help too. He was older than Mama and functioned as her protector. He didn't agree with her struggles and often argued with her about it. Still, when we were all together, I could see that Mama was trying.

We had already been through so much, but Mr. Mark gave us a sense of stability. He would pick us up from school, and sometimes we would stop at Sonic. My brother always got a hot fudge sundae. Mr. Mark and I would get pineapple or strawberry. Mama would sometimes get one too. He loved Al Green, and his music was always played in the car. I loved everything about him.

After about a year, things between him and Mama changed, and we moved to a house on Dutel Street. But he never stopped showing up for us. He still picked us up, brought us donuts, and checked on us. One morning in 1999, everything changed. My brother and I were getting ready for school when Mr. Mark and Mama walked in. He had a box of fresh donuts. Mama seemed rushed. He leaned against the couch, struggling to breathe. Mama quickly left to get his inhaler. We panicked—but we acted fast. We grabbed my brother's nebulizer and helped him use it. Within minutes, his body began to weaken. Mama returned—but it was too late. Mr. Mark had passed away. We were devastated. Watching someone I loved die in front of me changed something inside of me. After everything we had already been through, this moment hardened me in ways I didn't understand at the time.

Chapter 7: Elementary School

When I was younger, I attended two elementary schools, Meaux Elementary and Herod Elementary. Meaux Elementary was outside the city limits, with very few Black students. My family was well-known in the area because of my grandparents' farming background and my grandfather's cement company. I was often the only Black student in my class. I didn't feel out of place—but I was aware. Most of my classmates were kind, but one experience stayed with me. In second grade, my teacher made me read aloud from a lesson about slavery. It felt intentional. It made me uncomfortable—and to this day, I still question her motives. Later, we moved and I attended Herod Elementary.

That was a major culture shift. There was more conflict—fighting, bullying, and disrespect. I wasn't used to that environment, and it scared me. I would cry sometimes because I didn't know what to expect. But my fourth-grade teacher had an influence. She was strict but caring, and I felt safe around her. Eventually, I adjusted and began making friends. By fifth grade, I felt more comfortable. Even though life outside of school was difficult, I always did well academically. Until one day, I got into my first fight with a close friend over a jump rope. We both ended up in detention. But even then, we laughed, joked, and eventually became friends again.

Chapter 8: Friend Turned Sister

My first fight was with a girl named Mindy. Out of that fight came a bond that lasted an exceedingly long time. She was much shorter than I was, but that did not stop her from swinging at me. At school, we were in the same class and were always talking to each other about whatever the teacher said. She stayed cracking jokes, making funny faces, and getting everyone off task. I enjoyed being around her because she became an escape from everything going on at home. We were always getting paddled, put out of class for giggling, or made to kneel in front of the whole class. That is when I realized we were inseparable.

After school, we were like Siamese twins. There was no me without her and no her without me. I was at her house every single day and night because it was only a three-minute walk from our house on Dutel Street. Her parents were so loving and never minded me being there. Every day, she would ask if I could spend the night. They made sure I was fed, clothed, and taken care of. I went to Bible study and church with them, and I even joined them on fishing trips. Her cousin, who was a licensed beautician, always did my hair. We usually got similar styles, and people started saying we looked alike. That was probably because we were always together. We made many trips to the corner store for boudin and hot chips. That became our routine anytime we had money. My friend had four other siblings, and they treated me like I was their little sister too. They took me in and allowed me to live with them for a school year while my brother remained in the house on Dutel Street. They were the kindest family anyone could ask for. I never went without. Everything my friend had, I had. Without a doubt, her family saved me from enduring much more than I already had. To this day, they still consider me family. I was honored to be her maid of honor at her wedding, and that meant everything to me.

Chapter 9: Dance Battles & Rapping

Being with Mindy came with a lot of fun and entertainment. Her cousin, whom we called Coach C, was well known in the city for his dedication to helping young people. He had a dance team called the Favorite Dancing Cats, or FDC, which performed choreographed routines for the yearly festival. The team had more than fifty kids. It was a way to keep us active and out of trouble. The dance team competed against other teams, and eventually my brother, Mindy, and I all joined. Before the fall festival started, we practiced after school constantly. Every move had to be perfect. If we did not get the routine right, we had to run until we did. Sometimes I would mess up on purpose because the consequences made everybody laugh. Coach C would say the wildest things when we were off beat. One time, when I could not get a routine right, he yelled, "What are you doing? You're moving like Esther on *Sanford and Son!*"

Even though we had a wonderful time, we knew he took it seriously. If someone from another dance team walked by, we would stop practicing because we thought they were trying to steal our moves. Then we would break into our signature chant and routine, walking in unison, twisting our bodies, twirling our hands at our sides, and yelling, "Here comes the FDC — uh oh!" Every year, we had uniforms made, usually pleated skirts with airbrushed shirts for the festival. Everyone looked forward to seeing our outfits and routines. It was almost like a battle of the bands, except with dancing and chants about how we were the best. Of course, part of the fun was getting under our competitors' skin.

Coach C was passionate about everything he did for the youth. In addition to the dance team, he also had a baseball team. But he did not stop there.

Eventually, we even started a rap group. The group was called LA Soldiers. I was Lil B. Along with me and Mindy, there was another girl and three boys. We recorded multiple songs and had the chance to perform in front of large crowds. Atlanta was one of the places we got to perform. There were several record label representatives there to watch and judge us. We gave it our all and hoped for a record deal. Unfortunately, that did not happen, but they liked us. And if you're wondering whether I enjoyed rapping — I absolutely loved it. As I mentioned before many of my peers were in similar situations, but Coach C gave us something positive in the community to look forward to. And his efforts will go down in history.

Part Two: *Cracks In the Ground*

Chapter 10: A Breath of Fresh Air

Around this time, we were becoming teenagers. Our dad finally removed us from an environment filled with uncertainty. We moved in with him and our stepmom, who were married by then. They bought a beautiful home for us. My brother and I each had our own room. That was exciting. Even so, I still felt reserved because we were away from our mom. Although she had become more functional and had started working, she was still using drugs, just in a more controlled way. We changed schools and began living a much more comfortable life. Still, everything felt foggy to me. I became rebellious toward my dad and stepmom. They were extremely strict, and that took some getting used to. But I knew their rules came from love and from wanting what was best for us. The family member we had lived with before had been harsh and seemingly uncaring. My dad and stepmom were different. They made us feel loved, secure, and wanted. We had birthday parties, Christmas gatherings, and our hair and clothes were always taken care of. We were living a completely different life. I started to see what a family was supposed to look like. We were finally getting the attention and care we needed.

Everything seemed perfect, but I still missed my mom terribly. I worried about her all the time. Even though she was only twenty minutes away, it felt like she was far from me, and I wanted to be close enough to watch over her. She called often. I would cry and beg her to come get me, and she would promise that she would.

Chapter 11: Let Freedom Ring

I was only one phone call away from being back with my mom, and eventually she got settled into her own place. It was not the best environment, but I was on my way back to her. My dad and stepmom were not happy about letting me go, but my mom had shown enough improvement for them to allow it. My brother stayed with our dad. But me? I hauled butt. I was desperate to be under the same roof as my mom again, even without fully understanding the environment into which I was stepping.

We lived in what we call projects, which was the second of the two we lived in. It was loud, chaotic, and somehow fun at the same time. My older cousins, Jenny and Jan, lived there too. Their dad, my Uncle Tim, had a separate apartment nearby. I became remarkably close to them, so when they came back from Chicago, it felt like a family reunion. Their apartment was in the first building right in front. Across from it was a small mom-and-pop store where all the dealers hung out. It felt like a block party every day. Even though I was only thirteen, I felt free. And I was. My mom was nowhere near as strict as my dad and stepmom. She let me roam with my friends and older cousins all the time. As long as I went to school, she did not question much. I got into a few scuffles and, for some reason, became ready to fight over almost anything. I hate to admit it, but I did not mind fighting every now and then. Somebody eventually nicknamed me Miss Tyson because they kept seeing me fight. My cousins grew up in Chicago most of their lives, so you can imagine how they managed conflict. We did not back down from anything.

Along with that freedom came a lot of attention from boys. They were everywhere. I found myself drawn to the "drug dealer" image — gold teeth, fresh sneakers, and nice cars. It felt like there was some magnetic pull between those gold teeth and my immature little heart. My cousins were beautiful, stylish, and always had people around them. Because they were from Chicago, people were drawn to them. Their style stood out. Their clothes were always coordinated. I remember Jenny wearing bright orange socks with a matching shirt and nail polish. It was obvious they had a different kind of style — a city style. Their personalities were different too. They were friendly, but they did not tolerate drama. Because Chicago had such a reputation, people seemed both intimidated by them and fascinated by them. They carried themselves in a way that stood out, even down to their accent, which was nothing like the way people talked in Louisiana.

During that time, I saw a lot. I saw different drugs, broken mindsets, and just how shameless and demoralized people could become. Arguments and fights happened all the time. Nobody cared what anyone thought. It was like everyone shared the same mentality. Nobody felt better than anyone else. Everybody believed they were doing fine. Everybody seemed comfortable in the lifestyle. The routine was simple: school, work, and the club on weekends. I ended up babysitting my cousin's child so she could go out with her friends. At thirteen, that did not seem like a big deal. I had already been taking care of people for so long that it came naturally to me. Eventually, I began taking advantage of my mom's leniency. For most teenagers, that might be normal. But in my situation, being exposed to so much did not work in my favor. I began to mirror the people around me. Things became easier for me to do because I did not have an authoritative parent watching me, and everything was right in my face. It felt like I had no choice but to fall in line with what everyone else was doing. My only escape was the eight hours a day I spent at school. Oddly enough, the people I was around outside of school were completely different from the people I saw in school. There was a strange balance in that.

Chapter 12: No More Bullets

Living in the kind of environment I described in the previous chapter came with many unknowns and many dangers. Because I spent so much time with my cousins, I witnessed them go through a lot themselves. One particular night changed my life forever. I was over there one night, possibly babysitting, when an argument suddenly broke out and turned physical. My cousin Jan was pregnant at the time, and her boyfriend was abusing her. She yelled, "Parker J., call the cops!"

I ran downstairs to the neighbors and called 911. I told the police my cousin was being abused. I was terrified, but I wanted to help. I was only thirteen, so there was only so much I could do. Feeling proud that I had done something to help, I went back upstairs and yelled to her boyfriend that I had called the police. I said it with a little attitude too, which probably made him even angrier. I thought he would leave. Instead, everything got worse. He pulled out a gun and said, "Oh, yeah? You called the cops?" Then he started shooting at me.

I did not have enough time to run down the stairs, so I jumped off the balcony and landed on the ground below. He ran downstairs after me and got closer. I was lying on my back in the mud while he stood over me, still shooting in my direction. It was raining, and I could not find the strength to get up. I could hear bullets hitting all around me. To this day, I still do not know how I survived without being hit. Eventually, the shooting stopped. I do not know whether he ran out of bullets or something else made him stop. But when it finally went quiet, I got up and ran to our apartment to tell my mom what had happened. It felt like I was in a horror movie, trying to escape a killer.

My mom pressed charges, but he was never arrested because he went into hiding. For a long time, I lived in fear that he would come back and finish what he started. Then one day, while visiting Jan, I heard what had happened. She was near the end of her pregnancy when police tried to stop him because of the warrant connected to what he had done to me. Instead of surrendering, he led them on a high-speed chase. He crashed into a tree and died from his injuries. When I heard the news, I felt relief — and a little remorse too. God was with me the night of that shooting and every day after. I know without a doubt that I was protected.

Chapter 13: Teen Court

Because of the many physical altercations I got into, I eventually found myself in the back of a police car. After a few court dates, I was sentenced to teen court. Teen court was a program designed to redirect youth offenders and help prevent juvenile incarceration within the parish. Once sentenced, you had to appear in court with a parent and be judged by your peers—other teens who were also in the program due to their own misbehavior. I don't remember exactly what my sentence was, but it ranged somewhere between six months to a year. During that time, I had to complete group projects, take part in activities, judge new offenders, and attend field trips. I had to show up every Wednesday evening. Eventually, the roles reversed, and I became one of the ones helping to judge others.

The program taught us accountability. We worked in groups, traveled to the Lafayette location, and took part in different activities. I have to admit; I actually looked forward to going. There was a lot of joking, laughing, and playing around when the time allowed. Even though it felt like fun, the program profoundly changed my life for the better.

Chapter 14: Hospital & Cartoons

We continued living in the projects while I finished middle school and went through high school. I met a boy named Luke through the rap group I was part of, and he eventually became my boyfriend during my last year of middle school. We spent a lot of time together—dressing alike, going to festivals, teen dances, and even church. We dated from the time I was thirteen until I was about sixteen. During that time, I became pregnant.

At fifteen, I gave birth to my beautiful daughter, Lila. I named this chapter "Hospital and Cartoons" because I was still a child having a child. It may sound cliché, but it was my reality. When the nurse came into the delivery room to give me medication, I was watching cartoons. She looked at me in disbelief. I don't know whether it was because of what I was watching or because I should have been watching cartoons instead of having a baby. My mom and my boyfriend were there with me through the long labor. After twelve hours, I finally delivered my baby girl. Her father was overjoyed. He couldn't stop smiling. At first, I felt ready. I was eager to take on the responsibility. But after the delivery, reality began to set in. The nurses allowed me to rest, only waking me to feed and change my baby. But soon, I realized this wasn't temporary. I had a life to care for—my own child. When it was time to leave the hospital, I felt it all hit me at once. As I walked toward the exit doors, my heart sank. A deep wave of depression came over me. I started thinking, what have I done?

When I babysat my cousin's child, I could always give the baby back. But this time, there was no handing her over. This was my responsibility now. The depression lasted for over a month. I had broken my mom's trust. I hadn't been honest about being sexually active, and because of that, I wasn't on birth control. My mom struggled with her own feelings about it too. I didn't know what I was doing and depended on her for everything. Thankfully, because I was a first-time mom, the health department sent a nurse to our home at no cost. She taught me how to care for my baby. That was one of the best things that could have happened to me.

I began to feel more confident and less like a burden. With her help—and my mom's determination to see me finish school—things slowly became easier. I even started braiding hair to make money so I could buy diapers, wipes, and clothes, since I was too young to work. My daughter, who many say looks just like me, became my best friend. She respected me as her mom, but she also supported me in ways I didn't expect. She cheered for me during my basketball games in high school. She reminded me that everything would be okay. And in time, it was.

Chapter 15: The Leather Heart

Throughout most of my high school years, I played sports—mainly basketball. I won't say I was the best player, but I definitely made an impact on the court. I understood that there was no "I" in team, and my role mattered. I wasn't focused on scoring points. My goal was to stop the other team from scoring. Defense, rebounds, and blocked shots—that's what I took pride in. I even found old newspaper clippings from those days. While I did score at times, my strength was always on the defensive side. During my senior year, I was awarded All-Defensive Team in our district. I've always loved basketball and still have a desire to coach one day. Naturally, being a starter on the team led me to date the star player on the boys' basketball team. I had known him since middle school. We were just friends back then. He had recently moved from East Louisiana. He was extremely athletic and was even part of the dance team. His athleticism, bright smile, and confidence drew a lot of attention—and I was one of those girls drawn to him. Everyone believed he would go on to play professionally. He was that talented, even at the college level. What made him special to me was what we had in common. I didn't fully understand his background until we started dating, but once I realized we shared similar struggles with our mothers, I connected with him on a deeper level. He became someone I leaned on.

After I broke up with Lila's father due to abuse, Cody stepped in and helped me with my daughter. His grandmother also supported me. I spent a lot of time at their house. We lived close to each other in the projects, just a short distance apart. We shared meals, missed the bus together, and were often late to school together. We talked about getting married one day and believed we would be together forever. At that time, he had never met his father. Because of my natural instinct to help and heal others, I took it upon myself to find him. After searching online, I found a phone number connected to his father's last name. I called—and reached his grandparents. Eventually, his father came down to meet him for the first time. We even spent a weekend visiting them. It was a meaningful experience. He got to meet his father, grandparents, and other family members. They stayed in contact, and he began building a relationship with his dad. That moment meant a lot to me. Even though my own life wasn't stable, helping someone else find healing gave me purpose. It showed me that I could do something meaningful—and that realization stuck with me.

Chapter 16: The Clinic

After graduating high school, I had a plan—for myself and for my daughter. I enrolled in college away from home and was accepted into a nursing program. My parents helped me secure an on-campus apartment. I was on track to become a registered nurse. But I was hiding something. I was pregnant again. When I told my parents, they were devastated. They told me they would not continue to support me unless I had an abortion. At the time, I wasn't completely against it. I wanted my education. But I also wasn't fully convinced. My dad gave me a check and told me to take care of it. I went to the clinic for the first appointment. I didn't realize it was a two-step process. The first visit included counseling, an ultrasound, and a video explaining the procedure. Sitting in a room full of young girls, I felt fear take over. I had just seen my baby on the screen and now I was watching how it would be removed. Outside, protesters were shouting and holding signs.

Something didn't sit right with me. I went home unsure. I delayed the second appointment for a couple of weeks. Eventually, I went back. During the ultrasound, I could see small features forming. I had already made up my mind—or so I thought. While I was in the back, my mom was at the front desk with the check. I didn't know what was being said. When I came back out, the clerk quietly told me, "Baby, you're too far along." She handed the check back. I broke down crying. Years later, my mom told me the truth. I wasn't too far along. She had asked the clerk to tell me that. My mom didn't agree with the decision, but she was trying to support me the best way she knew how. The clerk agreed with her. I went on to have my second daughter, Lacy. I didn't attend

the college I originally planned to, but I enrolled in a
local college instead.

Part Three: *Falling and Fighting*

Chapter 17: Prove Them Wrong

Naturally, people had something to say about me being a teenage mother of two. But truthfully, no one was surprised. Many blamed my mom because of her past. In their eyes, everything was her fault. But I knew better. The decisions I made were mine. And I had to fix them. I was determined to prove everyone wrong. As I continued through school and raised my daughter, I learned how to manage life with the help of those around me. She eventually enrolled in Head Start during my senior year, which helped tremendously. I stayed focused, played basketball, and graduated with my class. After that, I had something to prove.

Ten days after giving birth to Lacy, I started attending LPN school. I was so determined that I did not wait the respected time to heal properly after giving birth. I was elected class president—something that surprised me, especially being the youngest in the class. I graduated with honors and immediately started working at a geriatric facility. At twenty-one, I became a CNA supervisor. It wasn't easy managing different personalities and age groups at such an early age, but I managed it. I continued working as a nurse while also teaching at a small college during the week. I explored different areas in the medical field, including working in a psychiatric facility and a prison. Through those experiences, I gained a deeper understanding of people—and a stronger appreciation for how far I had come. I realized just how blessed and favored I truly was.

Chapter 18: Mistaken Identity

Everything was working in my favor. I was working two jobs, had a good career, and my children were doing well. Then suddenly, everything took a turn. One day, I was carrying groceries up to my upstairs apartment when a man named Joseph approached me and offered to help. He was very charming and seemed masculine and confident. I noticed the tattoo beneath his left eye—a teardrop, which often symbolizes a gang-related murder. His teeth had a pretty gap, and he smiled from ear to ear. I was caught off guard by his strong, helpful, yet thuggish demeanor. I hoped the tattoo did not mean what I thought it did, because I was not attracted to that type of man. Even so, I overlooked the possibility and gave him a chance. That decision came with dangerous consequences.

He was no stranger to the criminal justice system and dating him turned out to be one of the most unwise decisions I had ever made. As the months went by, I began to see his anger and mental instability. I tried to fix him because I liked him so much. His background felt familiar to me. He was a popular, well-known drug dealer, and people respected him everywhere we went. I also believed no one would ever physically harm me because he was not afraid to use force to protect those he loved. Still, I ignored the signs.

Eight months into dating, he asked me to marry him. We went to the courthouse, signed the paperwork, and were married by a justice of the peace without my parents—or anyone from my side of the family knowing. His family was there: his mother, sister, and brother. Marrying someone so familiar to my past was not wise at all. The very same day we got married, he grabbed my phone and searched through it, looking for anything he could use against me. He became controlling instantly. I mentioned that he was physically protective but imagine believing your husband will defend and protect you, only for him to beat you for all the wrong reasons. I was being abused and did not even understand why. Everything began to fall apart almost immediately after we said, "I do." He also used cocaine, which I did not know at first. Later, it explained so much of his aggression. He would get angry over the smallest things.

One day, after I had worked a sixteen-hour shift, he picked me up late on purpose because we had been arguing. He had even threatened to leave me at work. On the drive home, I complained because I had let him drive my car that day, and I was exhausted. Because I was complaining, he hit me across the face with the back of his hand while I was sitting in the passenger seat. I screamed and saw blood everywhere. My nose was pouring blood, and my left eye swelled shut almost immediately. I was too afraid to call the police.

After that, I paid close attention to his demeanor. Once his jaw clenched and I could hear his teeth grinding, I knew he was angry and that some form of abuse was coming. I finally understood how people in abusive relationships begin to feel trapped. I felt like I could not escape, yet I still hoped things would get better. Not only was I being physically abused but I was also being emotionally abused. I still remember the things he said to me. Even so, I kept managing the household and my career.

I had always heard that one decision can either build your life or wreck it. Unfortunately, I had to learn firsthand how devastating a wrecked life can be. Another piece of advice I had heard was that one of the most important decisions you will ever make is who you choose to marry. That was true. I thought I could hold everything together and hide it from the people who loved me—until the day the police showed up at our door. Someone had reported suspicious drug activity inside our apartment. The police searched the home and found drugs, including crack cocaine and marijuana, which I knew were there. We were both taken to jail and charged with multiple felonies, though we later bonded out. It was my first time ever going to jail. For him, it was not.

Walking into the parish jail is not a memory I cherish. I was held in booking with him, though we were separated by two rows of chairs. Every so often, he would turn around just enough to whisper, "Stop crying, or they'll think you're crazy and put you in solitary confinement." So I tried. I tried to swallow my sobs, to quiet the trembling in my chest, to nod as if I understood how to hold myself together in a place that was already breaking me apart. An older Black female correctional officer was taking our pictures and fingerprints. She noticed my tears, looked up at me, and said, "Don't cry now. You weren't crying when you had drugs in your house." Her words hit me like a slap. Whatever strength I had been trying to gather dissolved, and I cried even harder. Then another female officer took me to be strip-searched. I was terrified, bracing myself for the kind of degradation I had only ever seen in movies. But she was gentle. She did not humiliate me. She did not make me cough, bend over, or do anything drastic. Instead, she spoke to me with kindness I did not expect in a place like that. She told me I was going to be okay, and for a moment, I wanted to believe her. After that, she escorted me to the elevator, and I was taken to the fourth floor. There, I was led into a room to collect my belongings for the night: a plastic cot, a sheet, and a brown paper bag with a peanut butter sandwich, a packet of jelly, and a red apple. I was also given a roll of toilet paper, a miniature toothbrush, and a small tube of toothpaste. Because the dorm was overcrowded, there were no cells available to sleep in, for which I was actually grateful. I am extremely claustrophobic, so instead of being placed in a cell, I had to sleep on a cot on the floor. Strange as it sounds, that small mercy mattered to me. Then I was brought into a dorm full of female inmates. The room seemed to stop and stare as I walked through the doors. One woman was moving around naked after her shower, completely unbothered. Others laughed and joked with one another as if this place were ordinary, familiar, and survivable. And then there was me, standing in the middle of it all, trying to "pop my cot." That was what they called putting the thin fitted sheet over the plastic mattress. Apparently, there was a method to it, a skill everyone else seemed to know. But it was my first time in jail, and I had no idea what I was doing. I fumbled with the sheet, my hands clumsy and unsure, and that was when I heard somebody say, "Oh, she's never been here before." My struggle had already announced me. One of the women came over and helped me, and even in that place, that small act of kindness found me. But the fear never really left. Once I had finally settled in, the same woman who had been walking around naked looked at me and said, "Tomorrow, I want your lunch." I covered my face and cried silently, remembering what my husband had told me downstairs. In that moment, I felt small, exposed, and utterly alone. To this day, whenever I watch the cornbread scene in Life, I am pulled right back into that dorm, back into that fear, back into the helplessness of not knowing what would happen next. I was only in jail for about ten hours. But ten hours can stretch into something unrecognizable when you are afraid. Ten hours can feel like ten years when every minute is heavy with shame, confusion, and uncertainty. I still remember hearing the guard call out from the dorm door, "Parker, roll out!" I had no idea what that meant. Midnight had already passed when my name was called for release. It was my twenty-seventh birthday. And yet, even in one of the worst moments of my life, I was still paying attention to someone else's needs. As I packed up my things, I noticed a woman who did not seem to have toiletries. So I rolled my toilet paper over to her and handed her everything else I had been given during intake. Even there, in that place, stripped of dignity and certainty, I still wanted to leave behind something useful. Maybe that was my humanity refusing to let go of me.

The following Monday, I received a letter from the apartment manager telling me I had only a few days to vacate the property because of the arrest. At the same time, I had to respond to the nursing board regarding the charges. I was humiliated. I could barely process what I had allowed to happen to my life. I had married a selfish man. He even told the police the drugs belonged to me, trying to save himself. I did not know he had said that until later. Even so, I took responsibility for my choices, because I knew he had the drugs in his possession and I allowed myself to remain in that environment. This was the consequence of failing to set boundaries and put myself—and my children—first.

My nursing license was eventually suspended for over two years, and I could no longer work as a nurse until my license could be reinstated. I was devastated. He showed no sympathy whatsoever. When I cried, his response was, "This is what comes with it," referring to the drug game. From that point on, I worked different jobs just to cover expenses. My biggest priority was making sure my children did not

feel what I was going through. They never knew how
bad it had gotten.

Chapter 19: He Spoke to Me

At the time, my ex-husband Joseph was a musician and often performed at local nightclubs. He never invited me to watch him perform, and I knew why. There were always too many women around him. He loved the attention and entertained it, often sleeping with other women. One particular night, after having our son, losing my license, and being without a job, I felt completely overwhelmed. Once my children were settled, I grabbed my Bible and sat in my car. I read a few chapters and cried out to God about everything I was facing. I prayed for Him to remove anything and anyone that was hindering my walk with Him. That is when something came over me. I still cannot fully explain it, but it was unlike anything I had ever experienced. It was spiritual—divine. Not an audible voice, but something I heard clearly in my spirit. I was twenty-eight years old when I received this message: "You will never struggle again once you turn 30."

Some people may think I imagined it, but I know what I experienced. It was not human. I have never forgotten it. The strange thing is, I did not spend my days repeating it or trying to force it to happen. I simply kept living. At the time, we were living in a small apartment that was cheap and convenient, but too cramped for my growing family. I was unemployed and facing eviction. My husband was not making much money from music, and things kept getting worse. Eventually, I moved out and took my children back to my mom's house. Then my husband went to jail for eight months. That was when I started to feel the message coming to life.

The owner of the college where I had once taught called me back unexpectedly and offered me a job. It was a blessing. I was finally able to earn more money, save, and pay for the random drug screens required by the nursing board. At one hundred dollars, once or sometimes twice—a week, those screenings were expensive. That teaching job helped tremendously. As time went on, I adjusted to my husband being incarcerated. Eventually, he was released, and we reconnected. Looking back, I truly feel like God had already removed him from my life for a reason, and I made the mistake of looking back. He returned and resumed the same behavior— abusing me, selling drugs, and using them. There was nothing I could do to change him. I prayed for him constantly, just as I would for anyone, but he was unwilling to change himself. This time, leaving him again was easier. And I did.

Because I was living with my mom, I was able to work, save money, and focus entirely on my children. Then, in a very unexpected way, what God had spoken to me became even more real. Three months before I turned thirty, and two days after our three-year anniversary, my husband was murdered. We were still legally married, but we were living separately. I had seen him briefly on our anniversary. He was strongly against the separation. But two days later, he went to meet another woman outside the residence where he was staying. It was a setup. He was shot in the side and back while trying to run after realizing he had been lured into danger.

The day before he was killed, he called me repeatedly. We laughed and talked for hours. I was supposed to drop our son off to him the next morning around 4:00 a.m. before driving an hour and a half to work. He was excited to spend the day with our son. Ironically, he was killed around the same time I would have been dropping our son off. Looking back, I believe God was protecting both my son and me from what could have become a fatal encounter. It was not even the first attempt on his life by that same person. I also began to realize that God saw me getting emotionally close to him again. Since our separation, we had not shared many lighthearted moments, and yet there I was, easing back into old patterns—bringing him groceries, taking him to work, checking on him. I believe God intervened because Joseph was never meant to be part of my "once I turn 30" story.

Chapter 20: Construction Life

While I was teaching at the college for the second time around, one of my students told me on Thursday about a construction company hiring laborers for a new project. After making a phone call, she gave me the company name and address. Needing a higher-paying job badly, I called in to work the next day. Hopeful and nervous, I woke up at 5:00 a.m., got into my white Nissan Altima, and drove an hour and a half from Abbeville to Sulphur, Louisiana. That is how I found myself walking into the office of CB&I.

It was a hot, humid morning in the middle of August, and the line of applicants was unbelievably long. I walked right past the line because I had no idea how the process worked. The receptionist told me to go back outside and wait. As I got closer to the front, I noticed people throwing their hands up and walking away frustrated. At first, I thought maybe they had forgotten paperwork. Later, I realized they were being turned away because the jobs they wanted were already filled. The company had a first-come, first-served policy.

Once I understood that, I felt discouraged. Since I had no construction experience, the only position I could apply for was laborer, and those spots filled fast. Then the receptionist came outside and shouted, "If anyone is here for a labor job, all of the positions have been filled. Try again another time!" The two people ahead of me threw their hands up and left. Now I am first in line. She looked at me and asked, "What position are you applying for?" I told her, "Anything, because I didn't drive an hour and a half to leave without a job." She asked what kind of experience I had. I said, "Only nursing, but I'm willing to learn anything." She looked visibly frustrated by my persistence and said, "Let me see if I can fit you somewhere, but you don't have experience, so it's not guaranteed." When she came back, she handed me paperwork with laborer written in the job section and said, "Take this to the next building for your drug screen and orientation." I knew God was in the room that day because she had just said all of those positions were filled. After completing everything, I received my assignment and showed up at this massive site with thousands of other workers. They were building a chemical plant, and I was in awe of how enormous everything was. I will never forget my first day. I had used the last of my paycheck from teaching to buy steel-toe boots. I wore old jeans and long sleeves until I could afford better clothes. During orientation, I was given my hard hat, reflective vest, safety glasses, and gloves. I was ready from head to toe. My supervisor brought me and a few other new hires to our crew and handed us a trash picker and a magnet. My boots were cheap, and the pain was terrible. I had to walk across rebar, picking up loose wire and trash before a concrete pour. The only bathrooms were portable toilets. I had never really had to use those before.

At my first break, I went inside of one, called my mom, and cried. I told her I could not do it. But I had already quit my teaching job, so I had no choice except to push through. The crew I was assigned to was from nearby New Iberia. It was all men, and they were welcoming. Everyone joked around, but I was shy at first and did not know how to respond. Over time, I got more comfortable. Once they learned my last name was Parker, they did not hesitate to imitate lines from *Friday*. It was awkward, but funny. After about three months, I had grown close to all of them. I enjoyed being around them and wanted to do more—and earn more. I began helping with concrete pours and would sometimes show up at 2:00 a.m.

with my supervisor's permission, working until 6:00 p.m. that evening. Getting paid weekly changed everything.

The financial burden was finally starting to lift. After eight months of driving three hours round-trip from Abbeville, I was able to move into my own apartment just ten minutes from the job site. Eventually, I was moved from outside labor to the lunch tent. It felt almost like a privilege to work indoors with air conditioning. My job was to keep the tables and floors clean. Of course, the floors never stayed clean, but sweeping for ten hours meant job security, and complaining would get you laid off quickly. Later, I was transferred to the office trailers to keep those clean as well. By then, layoffs had started, and I constantly worried my name would be called. While I was there, I enrolled back in school and made effective use of my downtime. I would turn the janitor's closet into a makeshift office using boxes, bring my laptop, and do my assignments. Since I handled the office trailers used by HR, executives, and other administrative staff, I made sure everything was cleaned thoroughly before disappearing into the closet. My goal was simple: don't give anyone a reason to come looking for me. That only worked for so long. Eventually, they figured out what I was doing—and instead of getting upset, they praised me for it. When they needed me, they would knock on the closet door as if it were my real office.

Like all construction jobs, that project eventually ended. I was one of the last laborers laid off, and I was proud that I had lasted that long. After staying home for a while, I got called to another construction job building a power plant. I started again as a laborer on day shift, doing the same type of work I had done before. The site was smaller, which made it easier. Eventually, the labor crews were split between day and night shifts, and I volunteered for nights. Because I was organized and experienced with documentation from my nursing background, I was given responsibility for tracking timesheets. I became the spokesperson for the night crew and was often called into the supervisor's office to provide updates on our tasks. I also kept track of attendance and behavior issues. Most of the crew made the job easy for me, especially the West brothers. They were helpful and always full of jokes. Then one day, I showed up and was called to the office. They handed me a white hard hat. I knew white hats were for supervisors, not laborers. I was confused. Someone had recommended me for a promotion. Just like that, I went from laborer to supervisor over a crew of men, and my pay jumped from eighteen dollars an hour to about thirty-two. I could hardly believe it. I wore that hard hat with pride. It was one of the humblest, most rewarding experiences of my life—all because I refused to drive back home when everyone else accepted "no" as the definitive answer.

Chapter 21: Pre-Trial Intervention

If embarrassment had a definition, this season of my life would come close. After going to jail, having my mugshot circulated among people I knew, and attending court appearances, I was ordered to take part in pre-trial intervention. At the time, I felt like I did not need the program. Still, I do not regret it. I was never a drug user, but as a first-time offender charged with a drug-related crime, participation was required. I had to submit to random drug screens, attend substance abuse classes, stay out of trouble, and pay for the program myself. Thankfully, I was working construction by this time and could afford the fees.

The program lasted about eighteen months. Once completed successfully, the charges would be dismissed. I was determined to follow every rule so I could have a chance at practicing nursing again. After many drug screens and community service hours, I finally received my certificate of completion. I said I do not regret the program because I became remarkably close to my caseworker. She was professional, kind, and never judgmental. We would talk personally, almost like long-term friends. She truly felt that I did not belong in her office. Because I stayed compliant, she made the process much easier for me.

Chapter 22: Unfortunate Circumstances

Unfortunately, I was never cleared to practice nursing again. I did everything that was needed from me. The only mistake I made during my suspension was arriving too late for one random drug screen. Anyone who has worked construction at a plant knows it can take up to two hours just to get out of the parking lot. One day, I simply could not make it in time. I pleaded with the nursing board. I wrote letters and even sent graduation photos. By then, I had already completed my associate degree, just in case I chose a different path. None of it mattered. My caseworker with the board continued denying my reinstatement. For the first time in my life, I gave up. I felt many different emotions, but I knew that if I kept working, my family would be okay. Then, one morning on my way to work, a cement truck sideswiped my car and forced me off the road. The accident left me injured—not enough to be hospitalized, but enough to cause ongoing neck and back pain. Even so, I kept working construction. I did not let the pain stop me. I hired an attorney and went through treatment several times in an effort to relieve it.

Chapter 23: A Settled Blessing

Approximately two years after my car accident, I was awarded compensation. Receiving that kind of money felt like a dream come true. I never expected such a blessing. Thanks to my attorney's diligence, everything happened smoothly. The moment I held the check in my hand, I at once began planning what I would do with it. I went straight to the bank and deposited it. I paid off debt and covered the cost of my final degree. I was able to bless a few family members and friends as well. I gave my car to my mom because I had recently bought a new minivan with money I had saved from my construction supervisor position. With the settlement money, I was also able to pay off the remaining thirty-thousand-dollar balance on it. I was even able to visit Napa Valley for the first time with a friend. Driving through the vineyards, taking a hillside bus tour, and walking through Muir Woods was a phenomenal experience. To this day, it is still my favorite place to visit.

Grateful does not begin to describe how I felt. God brought me through a terrifying car accident involving a fully loaded concrete truck that sideswiped me on a busy interstate. Because of the size of that truck and the speed we were traveling, the accident could have been much worse. But He had a plan for me.

Part Four: *Becoming*

Chapter 24: Entrepreneur

During my time in construction, I developed a real enthusiasm for cleaning. I had always wanted to own a business, so while I was still working construction, I applied for an LLC. I designed and ordered my business materials, bought equipment, and began marketing myself as an independent janitor. I focused on residential properties and businesses, offering janitorial services wherever I could. I drove around dropping off business cards at rental properties, real estate companies, and local businesses. Unexpectedly, I gained many clients. During COVID, cleanliness became a major priority for businesses. At the same time, many people were losing jobs and could not afford expensive rental homes. Because of those hardships, I found myself cleaning an increasing number of rental properties. Before long, my business became one that rental companies relied on. They called often. I would load my car with equipment and take care of multiple rental properties throughout the city. It became overwhelming—but in an effective way. My two older daughters, who were twelve and fifteen at the time, even helped me. I was also hired by a bakery and given a set weekly schedule to clean there. That was when I realized how much I enjoyed being a business owner. So, I took a leap of faith and left my construction job. Later that same year, a hurricane devastated the city, and because of the aftermath, my business doubled. I continued running my janitorial service for a few years until I eventually became an oil and gas operator at a refinery.

Chapter 25: The White Dove

Being a social butterfly has never been one of my strengths. I am naturally reserved and shy. Still, I had always wanted to be part of a sisterhood—something that would help me step outside of my shell and surround myself with successful women. For a long time, I hesitated to apply to a college sorority and honestly did not think I met the standards of such an extraordinary sisterhood, but eventually I took the initiative. Their history and my personality aligned beautifully with Zeta Phi Beta Sorority, Inc.

After applying, I began the intake process. Since I had already completed my bachelor's degree, I was able to apply through the graduate chapter. During the process, I was given the name "Ms. ExquiZite"—in other words, beautiful. I never expected that name, but I gladly accepted it.

The beautiful, successful women who became my sisters are amazing. I have learned so much from them. Group meetings and activities were enjoyable, and being part of that sisterhood helped me become more sociable and gave me a true sense of belonging. All of my sisters are supportive and encouraging. We are the best, and our mascot—the white dove—is a fitting symbol of peace and harmony within our sisterhood.

Chapter 26: My First Foundation

Once I received my car accident compensation, I bought my first piece of land. The property was just outside the city limits. I moved quickly, made an offer, and the seller accepted it. It was a wooded lot, just under half an acre, in an old subdivision. After closing, I stood in front of that land and cried. Everything was starting to become real. I was finally in a position to build my first home. One of the best parts of the process was hiring someone to clear the land and begin construction. During the build, I stopped by every single day to check on the progress. I'm sure the contractors thought I was watching them too closely, but that wasn't the case. I was simply excited. Seeing each step unfold made everything feel more real. When the foundation was poured, I knew without a doubt that it was happening. The process took about eight months.

My excitement was so overwhelming that I even went out and bought a shed to place on the property just so I could fill it with home décor I had already started purchasing long before the house was finished. After picking my daughter up from school, I would often stop by local stores to look for sales on decorations and pieces for the house. Even though she would be tired after a full day of school, she still found the energy to help because she was just as excited as I was to decorate her room.

At times, that excitement even caused a little tension between me and the contracted company. About a week before I received my keys, I had already started getting small pieces of furniture delivered to the house. He repeatedly reminded me that while he understood my eagerness, I was not allowed to move anything inside until the final inspections were complete and closing had taken place. But in my excitement, I was a little rebellious. In the end, he understood, and he was just as excited to see the finished product.

During the framing stage, my children and I would stop by and write Bible scriptures on the wooden beams. They would even act out how it would feel to live there by pretending to wake each other up for school and yelling, "Get up and get ready!" That was one of the best feelings in the world. Seeing my children even more excited than myself touched my heart deeply.

Chapter 27: Water Revival and Spiritual Encounters

On June 18, 2023, I made the decision to be baptized. It was not a casual decision, nor was it made out of routine. It came from a deeper place within me, a place that had grown tired of carrying life in my own strength. The moment was personal, sacred, and long overdue. What moved me even more was that the push did not begin with me, but with my youngest daughter.

At just thirteen years old, she came to me and said she wanted to be baptized and become a follower of Christ. There was something so powerful about hearing those words come from someone so young. In a world where children her age are often pulled in so many different directions, she made a bold and beautiful decision to choose God. Watching her desire something so spiritually meaningful stirred something in me. It convicted me. It inspired me. It made me want to draw closer to God in a way that was no longer casual, but intentional.

My children and I had always gone to church. We attended Sunday services and, at times, midweek services too. Church was familiar to us. It was part of our rhythm, part of what kept us grounded. But this felt different. I realized that although I had been present in church, there was still a deeper level of surrender God was calling me to. I felt a need to be baptized again—this time as an adult, with a fuller understanding of what it meant. This baptism was not about appearance or tradition. It was about surrender. It was about dying to the parts of me that had tried so hard to survive without God and rising with the understanding that I could no longer live independently of Him.

As a mother, I knew my children needed more than my protection, more than my provision, and more than my words. They needed my example. They needed to see what it looked like to follow Christ not just in speech, but in surrender. No title I had earned, no success I had achieved, and no accomplishment I could point to would ever outrank the importance of giving my life fully to God. Though I was nervous standing before such a large congregation, something in me knew I could not let fear keep me from obedience. I needed to do it. And in that moment, I did.

Out of everything I had accomplished in life, that was one of the moments that made me proudest—not because people were watching, but because I knew Heaven was. I felt something in me begin to come back together. Not all at once, and not without effort, but enough for me to know I was no longer as disconnected as I had been before. I began to feel whole again. I knew there was still a lot of work to do within me, but I was ready. Ready to walk in a different light. Ready to live in a way that bore fruit. Ready to stop surviving and finally begin surrendering.

Looking back, I realize there had been many moments when God was trying to get my attention long before I fully understood what He was doing. There were encounters I could not explain and moments when strangers seemed to see something in me spiritually before I could see it in myself. None of those experiences felt threatening, yet each one left a mark on me. Each one made me pause. Each one felt like a whisper from Heaven breaking through ordinary life.

One of those moments happened at a car wash. I was washing my car when an elderly woman pulled into the space beside me to vacuum hers. She looked to be around seventy years old. There was something refined about her, something polished, as though she had lived a life of comfort, yet there was also something unusual about her presence that I could not explain. As I stood there holding the vacuum hose, she stepped out of her car and walked straight toward me. She never made any move to vacuum her car. Instead, she began speaking as if we were already in the middle of a conversation, saying things that seemed random, almost as though I should have already understood her meaning.

She came so close that the tips of our noses nearly touched. For most people, that kind of closeness from a stranger would have been alarming, but strangely, I felt no fear. I had spent years working in nursing, caring for elderly people, moving close to them, reading their faces, tending to their needs, so perhaps that was part of why I stayed calm. I asked if she needed help with anything, and she smiled and said no. Then, before I could turn back to what I was doing, she placed both of her hands gently on my face, looked directly into my eyes, and said, "Something about you is very special, and God has something special for you." I stood there frozen in disbelief. I had never seen her before. Under any other circumstance, I probably would have recoiled at a stranger touching my face. But her hands were soft. Her touch was calm. There was something almost comforting about it, even in the strangeness of the moment. And just as quickly as she had come, she was gone. She got back into her car and drove away before I could stop her. I wanted to ask her name. I wanted to know who she was, why she had approached me, and what she meant by what she said. But I never got the chance.

That moment stayed with me. Even now, I still wonder what she saw in me. I still wonder what moved her to walk up to a complete stranger and speak over my life with such certainty. I still wonder whether she was simply an unusual woman having an unusual day or whether God had sent someone to remind me of something I had not yet fully realized about myself.

Another moment came at a gas station. I was about to walk into the store when an older man, around the same age as the woman from the car wash, was coming out. I have always had compassion for elderly people, so my instinct was to reach for the door and hold it open for him. But before I could, he took hold of the door first and stopped right in front of me. He looked at me in a way that felt deliberate, almost piercing, and then he said, "Jesus loves you so much." It was such a simple sentence. So few words. Yet the moment held more weight than it should have for such a brief exchange.

Usually, when someone is coming out of a door while you are going in, it happens quickly. You step aside, smile politely, and move on. But this did not feel quick. It felt suspended. It felt as though time itself slowed down long enough for those words to land exactly where they needed to. I did not know him. I was not even in a city that was familiar to me. And yet he stopped me as though he had been sent with nothing else to do but make sure I heard that message.

At the time, I did not fully know what to do with encounters like that. I only knew they unsettled me in a way that did not feel negative, but awakening. They made me ask questions I could not answer. Why did these moments keep happening? What were they seeing in me? What was God trying to show me?

Looking back now, I no longer believe those moments were random. I believe they were holy interruptions. I believe they were gentle reminders

that even when I felt unseen, God saw me. Even
when I felt spiritually unfinished, God had not
abandoned the work He was doing in me. Even when
I was trying to hold myself together, He was reaching
for me through the ordinary moments of my life in
extraordinary ways.

Maybe those strangers were only passing
through. Maybe they never knew the impact they left
behind. But I remember. I remember the softness of
that woman's hands. I remember the stillness in that
doorway. I remember how both moments left me
feeling exposed and comforted at the same time, as if
God was pulling back the curtain just enough for me
to glimpse His nearness. By the time I stepped into
the waters of baptism, I knew it was not just about
one decision made in one moment. It was the answer
to many moments. Many nudges. Many quiet
invitations from God that had been meeting me along
the way. It was my yes to the God who had never
stopped calling me, even when I was still learning
how to listen.

And now, when I think back on that day, I do
not just remember the water. I remember the
surrender. I remember the breaking. I remember the
beginning. Because that was the day I stopped trying
to carry my life alone and finally placed it back into
the hands of the One who had been reaching for me
all along.

Part Five: *Reckoning and Healing*

Chapter 28: Consequences

The decisions we make can become heavy burdens—not only on ourselves, but on the people we love. Those choices can shift our focus and alter the course of our lives. We know what we know, and we often respond in the ways we believe are best at the time. Some people may not know what to do or how to do it. Still, I cannot ignore the idea that to make better choices, we must first recognize the harmful ones. The truth is, I made bad decisions on more than one occasion.

One of the biggest was having children who did not share the same father. I repeated harmful patterns without fully considering how disgraceful it might look or how damaging it could be to my children. Marriage before children is the goal for many people, and at one time, it was my goal too. Unfortunately, that did not happen in some of my relationships. Even so, I now recognize that those choices reflected selfishness and self-hate. I did not love myself enough to redirect the way I was thinking. Being a single mother became instinctive. I became numb to the idea of marriage. Independence felt safer. In fact, I often encouraged breakups because relationships no longer felt comfortable to me. I had grown used to living with just my children and me.

My preference became not having a man live in our home at all. I devoted myself so fully to my children that it still shows today. Their willingness to accept me having a partner is not strong, and I understand why. I created a household dynamic that centered around one parent. Still, the men I chose to have children with brought destructive consequences on their own, and in many cases, it was best for them to leave. But every decision came with a cost. Every action has an equal or greater reaction. To put it plainly, playing stupid games wins stupid prizes. That is a hard truth.

Raising children as a single mother was not easy, but I built strong relationships with my children. I was able to care for them and fill their lives with the Word of God. They can testify to my teachings and my desire for them to be better, to love themselves, to respect themselves, and to demand respect from others.

Chapter 29: Access and Egress

Anyone who has been through rescue training understands what access and egress means. I cannot help but relate those terms to my relationships. Access means being able to enter a structure. Egress means being able to exit it. That idea mirrors my past relationships because I made myself accessible to people who did not deserve access to me. I was trusting and believed it was love. I was not wise enough to recognize the pattern I had created. I was on a hamster wheel.

Not only was I repeating the same cycle, but more children came along in the process. Men would enter my life only to leave again, and that became its own pattern. No matter what, I kept finding myself creating the same irresponsible outcomes. I always wanted to feel a sense of belonging, yet I kept ending up abandoned.

Over time, I had to come to terms with myself. I needed to break the cycle that so many of us find ourselves trapped in. I had to learn to love myself and become accountable for my own actions. One day, I looked in the mirror and told myself repeatedly that I did not deserve to self-destruct, and that I was better than what I had allowed myself to experience. I can honestly admit that teaching myself not to be so trusting was extremely difficult. For some reason, I always wanted to help people and change their circumstances. But after realizing that everyone is not sincere, I began to pull back.

My disappointments were not only with men. I also had issues with friends I believed were genuine. Some of my friendships ended abruptly, with no explanation at all. That hurt me deeply—especially because I never understood why. No matter how many times I reached out to repair things, there was no reconciliation. Some people speculate that it may have been because of my success, but I hate to believe that. Ironically, the ending of two friendships happened during the same period when I was becoming the woman I am today. I became bitter while searching for answers. But I have learned to forgive and move forward. That may be one reason I have not entertained the idea of having another close friend. The feeling of abandonment is heavy, and if I keep allowing the same disappointments, the emotional cost will be high.

Chapter 30: The Mustard Seed Effect

I titled this book The Mustard Seed Effect because we all know what the Bible says about the faith of a mustard seed. Without question, my faith in God is the reason I was able to overcome so much. What fascinates me most is how exact the timeline of that spiritual message turned out to be. Two months before I turned thirty, my ex-husband was murdered. It took me time to understand both the timing and the reason. At times, I still question whether God was preparing me for a permanent separation from someone I was unequally yoked with, or whether it was simply an attack of the enemy.

But one thing I know for sure is this: once I turned thirty, my life began to look different. I never struggled again after thirty. Although my nursing career was over, my felony charges were dismissed and later expunged. My income from construction became lucrative. I re-enrolled in school because of everything that had happened with my license. I had been placed on a payment plan through financial aid because I had previously gone back but had not finished. The payment was only five dollars a month for a year. They wanted to make sure I stayed consistent, not because they needed the money. Once I had a record of consistent payments, I was given the green light to start again. I began working on my associate degree. My earlier credits still counted, so they transferred. I completed the program within a year and graduated. After that, I went back again for my bachelor's degree. I overloaded myself with classes so I could finish faster and graduated the following year. I missed graduating cum laude by only .04 points. That was disappointing, but I still finished. My children were present at both graduation ceremonies. When my name was called, I could hear them shouting, "Go Mama!" That meant everything to me.

Being able to pay for another degree was also part of God's plan. I enrolled in a fast-track process technology program at the local community college. The program was designed for those who had already earned an associate degree or higher. There was no financial aid available, but my car accident settlement allowed me to pay the eight-thousand-dollar tuition. The program was rigorous and demanding. I had to attend Monday through Friday. Thankfully, I did not have to work as much during that time because I was financially stable. I cleaned here and there, but nothing major. My focus was finishing.

That degree later helped me land a permanent position at one of the best refineries in Louisiana. I graduated from the program with honors and finally felt a sense of redemption after narrowly missing it before. Even so, getting hired was not easy. I applied at many places and never received a call for an interview. Until one day, I finally got my chance. I interviewed and was hired as an oil and gas operator.

My salary as an operator has truly been a blessing for me and my children. All the faith and courage I had to keep going helped shape who I am today. Even my poor decisions played a role in getting me here. We often try to separate the challenges from the blessings and focus only on the positive, but those bad choices redirected me toward redemption.

A close friend once told me that I had a testimony and that I could help change the lives of others. I believe that. I am here to tell you that God's grace is abundant. He held me close my entire life. For anyone who cannot understand what is happening in their own life, remember how much faith you truly need. Our priority should always be God. He loves us. He will never leave us or forsake us. He stays consistent even when we are not. I am living proof.

God also placed many people in my path for whom I will always be grateful. My friend's parents took me in and protected me from the unknown. My high school AP Biology teacher encouraged me as a young mother by inviting me and my baby girl to local book readings. Teen court taught me accountability. The owner of the college gave me another chance to teach, and through that opportunity I met a student who told me about construction. A receptionist gave me a chance in construction. God spared my life in a car accident while I was driving to work, and that accident later provided financial means that helped me move forward. Everything became a domino effect of blessings.

My mother was also delivered from drug addiction and became my support system through every high and low. She never went to rehab. Through faith and obedience, she was delivered. I could not be prouder of her. My parents continue to be my backbone. They are the best grandparents my children could ask for. My mother's love and commitment to her children and grandchildren prove that her past was never about wanting to destroy herself or her family. It was an attack, and she overcame it. My mom depends heavily on God for strength and guidance. You can see it in her daily life. On Sundays, she often attends two services—one at her home church early in the morning and another later service elsewhere. She tithes at both. Her love for God shows in everything she does. She calls me every day, and as soon as I answer, she starts singing gospel songs. I understand her reverence for God, so I let her finish before we begin our conversation.

Chapter 31: Where's Your Work?

Being consistent is key, and faith without work is dead. For a long time, I did not fully understand how simple and true that statement was. But after putting in the work, everything I had faith in began to happen. The "work" is often overlooked. We expect change through faith alone, while sometimes our egos convince us that we can succeed without any spiritual guidance at all. I do not agree. There is something uniquely powerful about success that is fueled by having faith in God. I have watched people accomplish a great deal without being spiritual, but often there is no joy attached to it. God-driven success carries a joy that is hard to define. It is not boastful. It is not prideful. It comes with deep gratitude.

I felt peace whenever I chose to pursue my goals. In the hardest seasons, reassurance would come over me again and again. A college classmate once told me, "Parker J., everything you said you were going to do; you did." I remember telling her that I wanted to join a sisterhood, build a house, and buy a foreign car. I did all of that within two years. I am not materialistic, nor do I believe a certain car proves God's will for my life. But it was one thing I had always wanted, and it stands as an example of how determined I am when I set goals.

Many people reach out to me asking, "What do I need to do to achieve your level of success?" My first question is always, "Do you attend church or have a relationship with God?" That question matters most because I must give Him the credit first. After that, I move on to explain the practical steps I took. I refuse to be a gatekeeper. But before anything else, I tell them to go to God in prayer. Human connections can help, but they are nothing compared to the power of God. Another question I ask is this: do you have the faith it takes to endure the most demanding parts of reaching a goal? And if so—where is your work? What have you done so far? Have you served others the way God commands us to?

One key practice that helped me was writing everything down and executing it. I made a list, checked things off one by one, thanked God in advance for what I was about to walk through, and thanked Him again after He brought me through it. That gave me the power to hope. I believe God wanted me to put forth the effort because He wanted me to feel His presence in the process. That gave me clarity and confidence—not just in myself, but in Him. I always remember this: faith in God first, followed by the work, produces promising results. Those two things must go together. One without the other is a setup for failure—or misery.

I must clarify that the work required to reach personal goals is not the only work that matters. There is also the work God calls us to do. Stewardship through generous giving, and the willingness to use our time, gifts, and talents to serve both God and others, lies at the heart of what it means when Scripture says that faith without works is dead. No matter how broken I was, I still found the strength to be a cheerful giver. Whether through tithing, inviting others to church, helping those in need, or encouraging someone spiritually, I understood those acts to be part of my assignment. I believe God did not bless me with a good-paying job simply for my own comfort, but so that I could be a blessing to others. More than ever, I am convinced that only what I do for Christ will last.

Chapter 32: Healing: I Know Who I Am

As I have mentioned before, authoring this book is immensely important—not only for those who read it, but for me as well. The writing process forced me to uncover painful truths about myself. It also became part of my healing journey. Going through life while burying anguish and repeating self-destructive behavior only minimizes accountability. To heal properly, I believe accountability is the beginning of a powerful process.

Lessons are revealed during the regurgitation stage of healing. I have learned that there were many choices I could have made differently—choices that may have made my life less painful. But as I said before, those same choices also pushed me to do the work. Even so, we do not have to be unwise in order to succeed. We do not have to destroy ourselves just to arrive at peace. But for those who have, honesty can still produce beautiful results. Acknowledging my flaws helped me identify who I really am.

Revisiting my past filled me with purpose. Joining forces with the Spirit of God gave me the ignition I needed to accept myself. Some people use success to cover up their truth and hide their skeletons. Doing that works against healing and self-love. Coming forward—saving myself from internal conflict—allowed me to help others too. I trust that my words will inspire healing in others and, in doing so, fulfill part of God's purpose for my own life.

Knowing my spiritual purpose means more to me than material blessings ever could. No matter how much money I may have in my possession, it will never compare to the fulfillment of feeling spiritually aligned. I know I may be labeled a "baby mama," a "teen parent," "the nurse who lost her license," or even a "fornicator." And while those labels may reflect parts of my life, they are not the whole of who I am. I still know who I am. I love who I have become. I love who God revealed to the world—both the good and the bad.

My mom used to tell me that I was my own worst enemy because I hated myself for a long time. I took those words personally. Today, that statement no longer applies. Instead of hating myself, I honor being me. Sometimes I sit in silence, admire myself, and say aloud, "Look at you. You go, girl!"

Chapter 33: God Gives Us Free Will: What Is to Blame?

This chapter was by far the hardest to write. It was incredibly difficult to put all of these answers into words. I understand that some may disagree with what I believe is to blame for my behaviors and decisions, but this is my truth. My family is made up of people who were clearly born with persistence and kindness. I do not believe environment created those traits. However, I do believe certain environments can draw them out.

Living in survival mode since childhood contributed to many of my successes. It made me a quick thinker and an analytical person. People have asked me why I was sexually active at such an early age—young enough to become pregnant. After reflecting, I have two clear answers. First, I was unwillingly exposed to sexual experiences and sexual stimulation at an immature age. That exposure increased during a vulnerable period in my life, and it caused me to gravitate toward relationships with boys. I thought that kind of relationship was the answer to feeling loved and wanted.

Second, I was afraid of being lonely after spending part of my life feeling isolated and emotionally abandoned. That fear contributed to my promiscuity, which in turn affected my choices in men. Once I moved back with my mom, I was surrounded by an environment where drug dealers were visible and admired. I became drawn to those types of men because of the lifestyle, the image, and the familiarity of it all. I dated—and even married—someone with those qualities without fully considering how destructive those decisions would be. At the root of it, I just wanted to belong causing me to idolize those types of relationships.

Even though I became a mother at an immature age, my maternal instincts were obvious. Good and loving parents raised me. I always wanted to be like my mom—kind, funny, loving. Because she gave us that side of herself, I became the same way with my own children, though I also carry some of my dad and stepmom's strictness. Providing my children with security has always been a priority.

I have also been asked how I managed to graduate from high school and complete college multiple times. The truth is, I was born with intelligence and persistence. My mom has many successful sisters and other relatives whom I watched closely for years. I believe our family is naturally gifted with intellect and perseverance. Success is expected of us. Going back to school and completing my studies came naturally to me. Still, I would be foolish to pretend that my circumstances also did not fuel my determination.

Many people compliment my cheerful outlook and my willingness to help others become better versions of themselves. I believe that part of my disposition comes from suffering. I understand what it takes to push through adversity. People often ask how I accomplished certain things. I can give them a list of steps, but I now understand that not everyone can follow the same list and get the same result. We are all wired differently, and we have all been shaped by different experiences. Just as people say, "You are what you eat," I also believe, "You are what you see." Exposure matters. Still, just because you were exposed to negativity does not mean you have to follow the crowd. And if you find yourself in disorder, it is never too late to change how you see life. Find the why of your actions —then make the necessary changes. No one said you cannot change your environment or reprogram yourself to be different. It takes work, but it is realistic.

Having faith in yourself may sound cliché, but I can testify that it matters. At the same time, we must remember that God gives us free will. So, change the narrative of your story. And do not be quick to judge, because no one truly knows what another person has lived through. In the end, reflecting and asking yourself what is to blame is the beginning of taking control of your own story. As children, we do not always have choices. But do not let anyone predict your future simply because they know where you came from or to what you were exposed. If you realize that a negative experience is shaping the way you behave, acknowledge it—and remove it from your path. We may not be able to change our genetics but learning how to suppress characteristics that do not benefit our lives is a superpower. I refused to let my experiences continue to be my downfall.

Chapter 34: Forgiveness

Waking up each day with a heart full of unforgiveness was only costing me my own peace and, in many ways, threatening my own salvation. I could never call myself a master of forgiveness because that would place me in the position of God, who alone forgives without measure. Yet I could not ignore the countless times He had forgiven me. When I began to imagine life without grace, mercy, and forgiveness from the Creator, I realized just how lost and empty we would be without them. That understanding changed the way I thought, and in time, it changed the posture of my heart. Forgiveness is not always easy, and it does not come without struggle, but it is a choice. In the end, it became the choice I made.

Forgiving my mother was one of the first acts of release I had to make. As I grew older, it became easier, because I began to recognize how closely my own decisions could have mirrored hers. I could not look down on her while ignoring the ways I, too, had fallen short. I had to confront the plank in my own eye before pointing to the speck in hers. Mama carried guilt for many years. Beneath so much of who she was, there always seemed to be an ache tied to the choices she had made. My brother and I found ourselves reminding her again and again that we were okay, that we loved her, and that we forgave her. Before authoring this book, I spoke with her openly about telling my story. She agreed and told me that sharing it might help other people. She also acknowledged that her choices were part of my story and accepted that I would speak honestly about them. That conversation left me with a sense of peace I had not realized I needed. It felt like permission, but even more than that, it felt like release.

Forgiving my ex-husband, however, required a different kind of surrender. It took more time, more prayer, and far more wrestling with my own heart. When it came time to prepare for his funeral, I found myself unable to grieve in the way I thought I should. After viewing his body, the reality of everything became heavy in a way that felt more overwhelming than sorrow. He had not kept up with his burial policy, so the financial burden fell entirely on those of us left behind. With help from a few of his family members, the checks from my construction job, and generous donations from my coworkers, I was able to give him a funeral and cremation. Even so, the weight of it all sat heavily on me. I could not believe he had left us with nothing to help carry such an unexpected responsibility.

I remember speaking with the funeral director, trying to explain the stress of planning arrangements while also trying to honor his family's request that he be buried instead of cremated. In her soft voice, she said, "Ms. Parker, I know this is a hard decision, but in reality, he did not live an extravagant life, so you should not feel pressured to give him an extravagant funeral. Do only what you can do." Her words gave me a measure of relief, but they did not remove the anger. I was angry at the way he died. I was angry that he had so easily fallen for the lie that he was meeting a woman. I was angry at the humiliation that seemed to follow even after death. Another woman he had been seeing before our separation came to the funeral. Because he was well known, social media filled with posts from women whose words and screenshots revealed pieces of his life I had never known. I sat through the service stoic and unmoved, my face flat, my heart hardened. Even as he lay in his casket, I was still angry with him. It took years before I could finally loosen my grip on that anger and choose forgiveness.

Then there was the suspect in his case. He was released and, to this day, has still not been prosecuted. When I learned he was out, fear settled over me. I cannot fully explain it, but I worried that somehow, he might retaliate against me. The ongoing court dates have been their own kind of burden, especially knowing that justice still has not been served for his children. One day, I saw him at a festival. In that moment, I told myself, do not say anything. Do not react outside of God's will. We looked at each other, and I gave a small nod. He nodded back. Strangely, in that brief exchange, the fear that had lived inside me seemed to lift. But even then, another emotion rose up in its place. I found myself wondering why he was free to stand there with his children, laughing and living, while my ex-husband's children would never again have that same chance with their father. That question stayed with me for a long time. Yet after nearly nine years of waiting for justice, I can honestly say that I have forgiven him too. I had to come to terms with the fact that final judgment belongs to God. There are some things no court can settle in the way the heart longs for, and there are some burdens I simply cannot carry without losing myself in the process.

My family and I are still close, even those whose actions left wounds behind. I genuinely love being around them. At some point, I made the decision not to let the discomfort of past experiences continue living inside my heart. Though I have not told all of them how deeply certain things affected me, the fact that I can sit in their presence without bitterness is proof enough that forgiveness has done its work in me. It is evidence that forgiveness is not weakness, nor is it pretending the pain did not happen. It is choosing peace anyway. It is deciding that what hurt me will not have the final word over how I live, how I love, or how I move forward.

Forgiveness not only made it possible for me to share my story with clarity, but it also released the anger I had carried and buried for far too many years. I believe forgiveness is one of the greatest acts a person can offer. Without it, true healing can never fully take root. I have continued building my life around that truth, especially after grasping the depth of God's love in giving His only Son so that we might have everlasting life. I came to understand that my joy could never be complete while resentment still occupied space in my heart. I know that hurt people often hurt people. I cannot explain every action, every failure, or every wound that was inflicted, but I do know that much of it was not of God. Even so, it is not my place to judge, condemn, or tear anyone down. My responsibility is to forgive, just as I have been forgiven.

As I have shared throughout this memoir, I lived through painful and unimaginable things, yet I chose to forgive everyone. That choice did not erase what happened, nor did it make wrong things right, but it did free me from carrying them any longer. I no longer avoid physical encounters or difficult conversations. I have learned how to live at peace with the reality of people's mistakes, even when I do not agree with their actions. I know not everyone has reached this place, but I can testify to the freedom that comes when forgiveness becomes real. I no longer long to see punishment returned for pain. Instead, I pray for healing, for myself and for those who caused harm—and for the kind of transformation only God can bring.

I may never understand every wound, every betrayal, or every wrong, but I no longer need to.

Forgiveness gave me something greater than answers—it gave me freedom. And in that freedom, I found peace, I found healing, and I found the strength to move forward without bitterness holding my soul hostage.

Chapter 35: The Right Way to Love

After learning how to forgive, I began to understand that forgiveness was not the end of my healing. Love was. I could not write about healing without also writing about love, because the two became deeply connected in my life. Forgiveness taught me how to release what had hurt me, but love taught me how to live again without becoming hardened by it. The more I read God's Word, the more I noticed how often love was spoken of in the Bible. It was not mentioned lightly. It was central. It was commanded. That alone showed me how significant it truly is. Healing required more than letting go of pain. It required learning how to love intentionally, even after life had given me so many reasons not to.

For a long time, it was easier to think about loving other people—or even trying to love myself—than it was to first love God the way I should have. But I came to understand that everything begins there. We cannot love rightly without first loving the One who created love. We cannot pour from a place we have never truly been filled. God commands us to love Him first, and then to love one another. Not when it is convenient. Not when it feels safe. Not when people deserve it. But with a love that reflects Him.

That kind of love is not easy. It asks for more than words. It asks for surrender. It asks us to love without conditions, without guarantees, and without always receiving the same in return. It asks us to extend grace to people who may never apologize and kindness to people who may never deserve it. Loving the people who hurt us in exchange for nothing does not come naturally. It comes only through God. I learned that the more rooted I became in His Word, the more the hard layers around my heart began to peel back. The bitterness that pain wanted me to keep started losing its grip. What once felt impossible slowly became possible through Him.

I also had to confront the things I had loved in the wrong way. I had to be honest about how easy it was to pour myself into things that made me feel valuable while ignoring what was actually eternal. Careers, money, recognition, and status can all become distractions when they start feeding the ego more than the soul. I know this because I lived it. At one point, I loved my nursing career so deeply that it became part of how I identified myself. It was more than a job to me. It was proof that I mattered. It gave me a sense of worth, accomplishment, and approval.

Looking back, I can now see that I had begun placing too much weight on something that was never meant to carry my identity. I was chasing acceptance, belonging, and validation in a place that could never fully satisfy me. I was trying to be seen, trying to feel important, trying to prove something. In many ways, I believe God allowed that part of my life to be stripped away because I had begun to love it too much. What I thought was purpose had started becoming pride. What I thought was passion had begun turning into idolatry. That realization was painful, but necessary. Sometimes we love things that cannot love us back. We become loyal to titles, careers, money, or recognition, and in the process, we neglect what matters most. We can begin loving those things more than we love each other, more than we love ourselves in a healthy way, and even more than we love God. But the acceptance we search for in the world is already freely offered in Christ. To love God, to walk in His commandments, and to surrender our lives to Him is to find the belonging we were chasing all along.

I learned that love, especially in our weakest moments, reveals what is truly growing inside of us. It is easy to love when life feels good, when people are kind, and when our hearts are not under pressure. But loving when we are disappointed, wounded, rejected, or exhausted is a different kind of obedience. It is the kind that produces godly fruit. It is the kind that transforms us from the inside out.

There was a time when I focused more on how people made me feel than on how God was calling me to respond. Pain has a way of making us self-protective. It teaches us to keep score. It makes us want to withdraw, shut down, or love with limits. But I came to see that love rises above offense. Love does not erase what happened, but it refuses to let hurt become the loudest voice in the room. Love has the power to outlive heartbreak, disappointment, betrayal, and resentment. Real love is not shallow, and it is not casual. It is not something to be thrown around loosely without understanding the cost. Love requires sacrifice. It asks us to lay down our pride, our grudges, our need to be right, and sometimes even our need to be understood. That kind of love is hard, but it is holy. It reflects the very heart of God.

The more I healed, the more I realized that my life would never truly be at peace if love was absent from it. Not performative love. Not convenient love. But real, unconditional, Christ-like love. I believe with all my heart that we would live gentler, freer, and more peaceful lives if we simply loved one another more the way God loves us. After forgiveness taught me how to release the past, love taught me how to move forward. And in many ways, that became one of the greatest signs that healing was truly taking place in me.

Poems: *Words From the Wise*

Promiscuity Without the Promise

Love at first sight when being so vulnerable

Will surely make you feel that it is honorable.

To give yourself to someone who seems so deserving

And the idea of being alone becomes unnerving

He makes you believe there is no judgment,

Until you're no longer needed, redundant.

He continuously pulls you in just for play,

Because you are unaware of the cycle that repeats
each day.

You began to repeatedly get left on "read,"

Not realizing that the relationship is dead.

And that sweet promise to become one…

It is a day that will never come.

All It Takes

Put down the phones!

Put down the gin!

The mustard seeds are sprouting again!

The faith you once had seemed to fade so rapidly,

And your only escape became the tap and "tree."

We have lost the faith that requires so little,

Because we've entertained what is harmful and brittle.

We've clung to things that serve no purpose,

And it was only designed to continuously hurt us.

The Love of Fire: Let It Burn

As I walked through the valley with nowhere to turn,

I felt the darkness along with a torturing burn.

The fire set me off to a desperate start,

That enabled me to eventually become set apart.

I have been labeled as an anomaly,

Because I used the fire to ignite the greatness hiding
inside of me.

Not understanding the path I was on at the time,

I chose to embrace the aches that would eventually
refine

The woman who was once lost, buried in shame and
guilt.

For I am now prepared to be a testament.

Emulsions: Battle Of the Flesh and Holy Spirit

In one containment the two meet

Without regards to possible defeat

Either one doesn't agree or comply

Making it difficult to accept or deny

There's too much friction for them to blend

So they fight one another until the end

We must trust in the Lord as we fight the battle

And choose to stay strong when our hearts are fragile

I advise to deny the flesh, accepting the Holy Spirit

Because our salvation will certainly depend on it.